Dear Parent:

Buckle up! You are about to join your child on a very exciting journey. The destination? Independent reading!

Road to Reading will help you and your child get there. The program offers books at five levels, or Miles, that accompany children from their first attempts at reading to successfully reading on their own. Each Mile is paved with engaging stories and delightful artwork.

Getting Started
For children who know the alphabet and are eager to begin reading
• easy words   • fun rhythms   • big type   • picture clues

Reading With Help
For children who recognize some words and sound out others with help
• short sentences   • pattern stories   • simple plotlines

Reading On Your Own
For children who are ready to read easy stories by themselves
• longer sentences   • more complex plotlines   • easy dialogue

First Chapter Books
For children who want to take the plunge into chapter books
• bite-size chapters   • short paragraphs   • full-color art

Chapter Books
For children who are comfortable reading independently
• longer chapters   • occasional black-and-white illustrations

There's no need to hurry through the Miles. Road to Reading is designed without age or grade levels. Children can progress at their own speed, developing confidence and pride in their reading ability no matter what their age or grade.

So sit back and enjoy the ride—every Mile of the way!

For Sue, Heather, and Drew.

And for Edy,
who gave me the confidence
when I didn't know "Beans"!

Library of Congress Cataloging-in-Publication Data
Torrey, Richard.
Beans Baker, number five / by Richard Torrey.
  p.   cm. — (Road to reading.   Mile 3)
Summary: When he is given an unlucky uniform number, Beans Baker
considers giving up baseball rather than face kidding from the other players.
ISBN 0-307-26335-5 (pbk) — ISBN 0-307-46335-4 (GB)
[1. Baseball—Fiction.   2. Self-confidence—Fiction.]
I. Title.   II. Series.
PZ7.T64573 Be 2001
[E]—dc21

00-034774
CIP

A GOLDEN BOOK • New York
Golden Books Publishing Company, Inc. New York, New York 10106

ISBN: 0-307-26335-5 (pbk)   R MMI
ISBN: 0-307-46335-4 (GB)

Beans Baker, Number Five

by Richard Torrey

The first game of the season
was only three days away.
Coach Munhall was
handing out uniforms.

Beans could hardly wait.
All spring he had dreamed
of wearing number 21.
Just like his hero—
The Great Roberto.

Coach Munhall held up
the number 21 jersey.
"Here I am!" shouted Beans.
But Coach Munhall handed
it to Sheldon.
"There must be a mistake,"
Beans said.
"That's *my* number!"

"No," said Coach Munhall.

"Here's your uniform."

Beans looked at his jersey.

"Number five? IT CAN'T BE!"

Everybody knew about
number five.
It was the number that
Wrong Way Haskins wore.
Haskins hit a home run in his
very first game in the majors.
But he ran around the bases
the wrong way.
Knowing he would be teased,
he quit baseball forever.

"Hey, Beans.
Make sure you don't put
that jersey on the *wrong way!*
Get it?"
Sheldon snickered.

"This is terrible,"
groaned Beans.
"I'm going to be laughed
out of town."
"It's just a number,"
said Coach Munhall.

At practice the next day,
Beans tried to hide his number
by wearing his jacket.
But it kept getting in the way.
It was his worst practice ever.

SWOOOOSH

"Hey, Wrong Way.

Let me show you the *right* way!"

said Sheldon.

He hit a pitch out of the park.

"Reminds you of The Great Roberto,

doesn't it?"

Beans told his friends he was
thinking about quitting the team.
"But you love baseball," said Lindsay.
"Almost as much as me!"
Beans shook his head.
"I can't play wearing number five."

"It's just a number,"
Chester reminded him.
"It's Wrong Way's number!"
said Beans.
"I might as well be wearing number 13!"
"Hey, that's *my* number!" said Chester.
"Sorry," said Beans.

Beans didn't go to the next practice.

"I'm not feeling well,"

he told his mother.

He wasn't really sick.

But when he thought about

wearing number five,

he did feel a little queasy.

At practice, everyone wondered

where Beans was.

"We can't let him quit,"
Chester said to Lindsay.

"How can we stop him?"

"I have an idea," said Lindsay.

"Here's the plan...."

After practice, Chester and Lindsay

stopped at Beans' house.

"Guess what?" said Lindsay.

"We're quitting the team, too."

"What?" said Beans. "Why?"

"We don't want to get

teased," said Chester.

"With these glasses, who knows

what other teams might call me?

Four eyes. Goggle head..."

"Goggle head?" said Beans.

"There's no telling what kind of
teasing a girl catcher might get,"
said Lindsay.
"Better safe than sorry.
Right, Beans?"

"WRONG!" shouted Beans.
"Who cares what other teams say?
Chester, your glasses
help you see the ball better.
Lindsay, you're the best
catcher in the league!
And you *love* baseball—
almost as much as me!
You guys can't quit just because
people might laugh at you.
You're making a huge mistake!"

"I think you just talked us
out of quitting," said Lindsay.

"I think I just talked *myself*
out of quitting," said Beans.

"It worked!" shouted Chester.

"I mean—see you at
the game, Beans!"

The next morning,
Beans and his family arrived
at the field just as the game
was about to start.

"You're late," shouted Sheldon.

"Did your dad go the *wrong way?*"

Coach Munhall made Beans
sit on the bench
because he had missed practice.
But he told him to stay ready.
Beans watched as the other team
went ahead, two to nothing.

Then, in the bottom
of the ninth,

Chester and Lindsay
both got hits.

With two outs, everyone
was counting on Sheldon
to hit a home run and
win the game.

"Come on, Sheldon!"

Chester yelled from second base.

"Just like in practice!"

"Only this time, it's for real!"

added Lindsay.

Sheldon's knees started to knock.

Even from the bench,

Beans could see his face turning white.

All of a sudden, Sheldon fainted!
He fell on top of the catcher.
R-R-R-RIP! went Sheldon's pants.
"Beans, you'll have to bat!"
yelled Coach Munhall.

RRRRRIPPPP

"NOW BATTING—

BEANS BAKER, NUMBER FIVE!"

said the announcer.

Beans' family cheered.

The other team laughed.

"Number five? It's Wrong Way!"

they shouted.

Beans stepped up to the plate.

"Hey, Wrong Way.

Want a map?" the catcher said.

Beans swung at the first pitch.

He missed, and his

helmet spun around.

"Strike one!" shouted the umpire.

The other team laughed even harder.

"Look!" yelled the pitcher.

"He's wearing his helmet

the *wrong way!*"

Beans swung at the second pitch.

He missed again.

"Strike two!" shouted the umpire.

"Maybe he's holding the bat

the *wrong way!*"

the shortstop hollered.

Beans took a deep breath
and waited for the third pitch.

KLIP!

Beans hit a ground ball.

It skipped toward the first baseman.

"*I'm out,*" thought Beans.

But the ball hit

the first baseman's knee

and bounced high in the air.

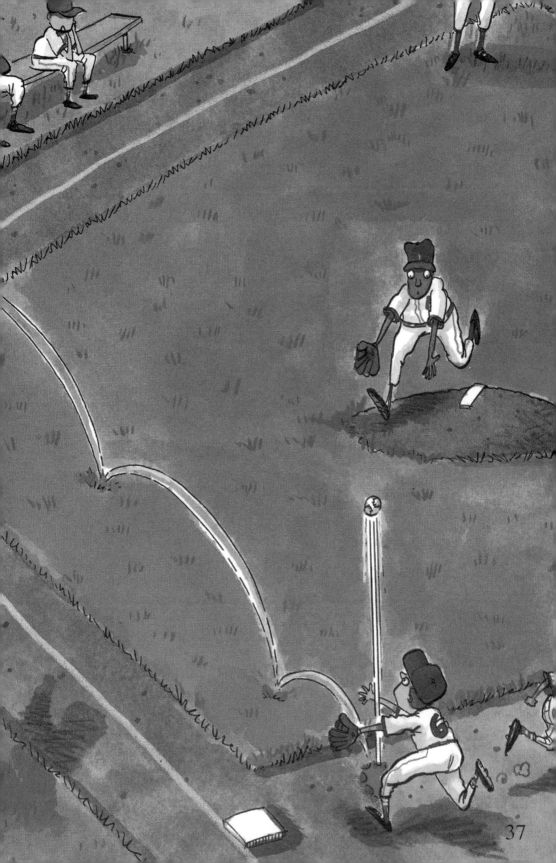

"Run!" shouted Coach Munhall.

Beans was already running,

rounding first base.

As the ball came down,

it hit the pitcher on the head

and bounced toward the outfield.

"Keep going!" shouted Coach Munhall,

waving his arm like a windmill.

Beans stepped on second base
and kept running.

The center fielder kept running, too—
right into the left fielder!

CRASH!

Chester scored!

Lindsay scored!

Beans tagged third base
and headed for home!

The left fielder picked up the ball
and threw it with all his might.
"SLIDE, BEANS, SLIDE!"
yelled Coach Munhall.

Beans, the catcher, and the ball
all arrived at the same time.
When the cloud of dust settled,
the umpire yelled, "SAFE!"

There was no more laughing.
There were no more
jokes about "Wrong Way."
Beans Baker, number five,
had won the game!
"Ice cream for everyone!"
shouted Coach Munhall.

"Hey, Beans," said Lindsay.
"Sheldon said he doesn't want
The Great Roberto's
number anymore.
Everyone's calling him
The Great RIP-erto!"

"Now you can switch
to number 21!" said Chester.
"No," said Beans.
"Five is fine with me.
Besides—"